STEPHANIE JT RUSSELL

ONE FLASH
OF LIGHTNING

A Samurai Path for Living the Moment

MJF BOOKS
NEW YORK

Published by MJF Books
Fine Communications
322 Eighth Avenue
New York, NY 10001

One Flash of Lightning
LC Control Number 2007926324
ISBN-13: 978-1-56731-861-6
ISBN-10: 1-56731-861-4

Printed in the United States of America.

MJF Books and the MJF colophon are trademarks of Fine Creative Media, Inc.

MV   10   9   8   7   6   5   4   3   2   I

In remembrance of my father,

Stephen Christopher Taddeo:

tender soldier, bootstrap philosopher.

And for Okuyama Sensei,

who always knew my footsteps from afar.

CONTENTS

ACKNOWLEDGMENTS

Grateful acknowledgment here to those who were nearby: to Frazier Russell, Bruce Joel Rubin, and Caleb Avery, for their incisive questions and sensitive insights; and to Margaret Lannamann, my detail editor at Ariel Books, for her caring enthusiasm and generous hours spent deliberating content, voice, and the finer points of deadlines. True Samurai, all.

Bowing now to the martial artists who have touched my life: Don Ahn, T. K. Shih, and my great friend Sifu Ken Lo, who never fails to understand. I am also indebted to Zheng Xian Wen, my treasured calligraphy teacher. Wherever he might be, I hope he is moved to exclaim, "Now, *that* is *art!*"

PREFACE

My book *Zen: A Spiritual Journey* begins with an anecdote. It's about an experience I had with my tea ceremony teacher, Yamada Sensei, in New York. One morning, I arrived at the teahouse in a state of considerable emotional distress. I was undergoing a very intense and demanding time. But I did not wish to call attention to myself. I wanted to subdue my feelings and get on with the class. I decided to arrive early and meditate. After a while, Yamada Sensei and another student came in. The teahouse is very big, but our class was in a small, three-mat *tatami* room. By the time class began, I thought I had my inner condition pretty well under control. I had summoned all my yogic discipline to ensure that no one would perceive my turmoil. For a time, we carried on the class in silence.

Then, out of the blue, Yamada Sensei turned to me and said, "You know, people think that when you practice Zen, you lose your feelings. This is not so. When you practice Zen, you laugh harder, and you cry harder." His self-knowing smile thawed every defense I had built up in my rigid misapprehension of spiritual discipline. It was perhaps the greatest kindness anyone had ever extended to me.

A few months later, I spent several weeks at the Oomoto School of the Traditional Japanese Arts, in Kameoka-shi, Japan. I was there to shoot an independent photo-documentary. This project was the reason I had studied tea ceremony with Yamada Sensei. On my second morning there, just after sunrise, I wandered the grounds alone to get a feel for the place and a sense of the locations I would be shooting. I came upon a building that was apparently a martial arts *dojo*. The spirit of the place began to reach me as soon as I approached the entryway. I slipped off my *geta* clogs and slowly entered the room.

At first, I did not venture in very far. The dojo's vastness was both physical and energetic. It faced a dense plum orchard. I found myself becoming mildly intoxicated with the perfume of ripe plums outside, mixed with the golden scent of tatami indoors. I do not remember when I walked to the center of the room. Nor do I remember when I sank to the floor in a relaxed *seiza* posture. A feeling of nearly drunken tenderness came over me. It was a complex elixir of feeling that blended into a simple sense of homecoming, as if I were in the company of a welcoming body of ancestors. There I sat in the empty dojo with tears drenching my kimono. I don't think my eyes closed once. Yamada Sensei would have been pleased.

Zen and the martial arts have touched my life for almost thirty years. But that is a longer story to tell another time. Here, at the start of this one, I want to share these two experiences, one in a New York City teahouse, and the other at a large dojo in a small Japanese township. Strange that I walked into a serene teahouse with my heart straining to perforate its shell of old fears; even odder perhaps, that I entered a dojo in Japan with that same heart, freed of its shell, shedding tears of joy and wonderment.

Freedom, for the true *Samurai*, is unself-consciousness in the presence of one's own truth. It is the discipline to end all disciplines, the love to begin all loves.

ONE FLASH OF LIGHTNING

*A Samurai Path
for Living the Moment*

忠　義

BEGINNING HERE

Mental calmness, not skill,
is the sign of the matured Samurai.

—Bokuden

Y ou are here, now, beginning to read this
book. You're on a chair or a couch, or maybe in
bed, enveloped in pillows and a blanket. Sunlight
or lamplight is striking the black type, making the
text stand out on the white page. You may be
aware of sounds outside your window—city
street traffic, or wind in country woods. Wherever
you might be, holding this book in your hands
and presumably reading these words is what
you're doing right now, right here. Within the
intricate landscape of your life, this activity may

be a very small thing. And the book itself is not necessarily the main point of this moment's particular meaning for you. You are reading it within the far wider context of your life. Like every moment, this one is a temporal thread within the greater weave of your existence, bearing the pure potential of the unknown. It doesn't matter if your present awareness is more keenly attuned to the book you hold, the sounds outside your window, or a fusion of everything that's going on around and within you. The point is whether or not you are truly awake to the moment, period.

Simple consciousness in the moment opens our senses to the epic nature of life, and our own part in it. That sounds big, and it is. But the immensity of this journey is quite modestly expressed in elusive details that compose the distracting sweep of daily activity. Those details of life, chiseled into sharp relief by simple awareness, teach the imminent truth of the moment. And deepening awareness arouses the mind to lucid veracity, stronger presence, and lessening fear.

This book visits the path of wakeful self-knowledge espoused and practiced by the legendary Samurai warriors, who transformed the course of Japanese history and, by extension, shaped early Western perceptions of Japan. This book is not a scholarly treatise on the soldierly arts of Samurai convention. Nor is it an academic reconstruction of military incidents, or directly political concerns, during the eras of Japanese feudal transition. Neither will I touch upon the subject of *seppuku* (ritual suicide). It does not relate directly to this book's purpose, and I feel the topic demands a discrete study of its own. Rather, the substance of this book is grounded in the spiritual under-pinnings of the Samurai martial construct, which supplied its adherents with a unique vehicle for uncompromising self-examination and trenchant personal development. I will approach the Samurai Code within the purview of its universal, ageless relevance to human nature, and specifically to our nature as seekers, a quality that transcends cultural and ethnic margins and binds us together in a single, common purpose—whether we are readily awake to it or not.

At face value, the orthodoxy of Samurai heritage bears little congruity to modern culture and psychology. Contrasted with Western cultural norms and precepts regarding the rule of law, feudal Japan appears a majestic and arcane alien reality. The austere, often brutal extremity of the Samurai Way is utterly removed from the have-a-nice-day social posture personified in the contemporary West. Even our casual greeting "How are you?" is rarely a bona fide question. It sets up a mutually complicit avoidance of real contact between people, and sanctions us to glide through the day without investing an ounce of ourselves in the true condition of other human beings. And never mind the even more alarming prospect of revealing our own sorrow, fragility, and imperfection. Or speaking the unvarnished truth, no matter what the consequences to our station in life. And just how pertinent is "How are you?" to the certitude of our own mortality, anyway?

Integrity, candor, and depth are human signatures that bridge the Samurai Way across centuries to a timeless truth of self-excavation and spiritual awakening. May the visceral poetry of the Samurai Code ignite in you an appetite for the heat of inner change. May one flash of lightning fix your gaze on the hard-won prize of a heaven unchained.

TODAY I DIE, LIKE EVERY DAY BEFORE

The "continually quick" are those who undertake an action quickly and settle the matter well.

—**Lord Katsushige**

Bushido, literally translated "Way of the Warrior," slowly evolved in Japan between the Heian and Edo ages, from the ninth to seventeenth centuries. As the guiding philosophy for the *Bushi* (martial artists) and Samurai (those who serve), this long-unwritten code was designed to guide the warrior in navigating the complex, often bloody, political and social turf of Japanese feudal society. Bushido directed the Samurai to cherish loyalty, courage, veracity, compassion, and honor above all else. The code was not crystallized into written form until the early modern period of the late sixteenth and early seventeenth centuries.

Beyond its pure military effect, Bushido had a galvanizing influence on the social norms that held Japanese society together. By the twelfth century, when the Samurai government was established in Kamakura, the Bushi had become more than a mercenary import; he was part of the de facto ruling infrastructure. Now a significant actor in the changing order, his incentives broadened: his role necessitated a deeper personal belonging within society at large. And while positioned in a nominally separate, elite class, his daily purpose involved scrupulous fidelity to the community in which he functioned as protector and overseer. In time, he grew to play a special part in the evolution of classical Japanese art forms. Devoutly creative Samurai became some of the country's great calligraphers, poets, and tea ceremony masters. Their public profile added weight to the cultural progressions that gradually instilled Japan's provincial people with a fully national identity.

It is important to note that Bushido's groundbreaking constructs did not vault full-blown from the mists of the twelfth century. Throughout the epochs of feudal rule, Japanese life was subject to intermittent phases of territorial combat, fraught with tension, risk, and trauma. Soldiers faced these brutal conditions with constant vigilance, as key players in a heated arena of high-stakes political rivalry. Along the way, the Samurai system, and its criteria for soldierly worth, underwent numerous structural and conceptual embellishments. But Bushido provided the essential continuity that kept the military engine running for seven centuries.

It took the better part of five hundred years for the Samurai Way to fully bloom. Ultimately, the warrior culture embodied the most significant social and philosophical expressions of Japanese feudal civilization. By the sixteenth century, vital principles of Zen Buddhism, Confucianism, and Shinto were coalesced into the unwritten code called *Bushido*.

In a classic Japanese paradox, Bushido's complex admixture belies the simplicity of the essential code, which is distilled into eight fundamental principles:

Jin:	*To cultivate a sympathetic understanding of people*
Gi:	*To embody and preserve meticulous ethics*
Chu:	*To evince loyalty to one's master*
Ko:	*To esteem and look after one's parents*
Rei:	*To show respect for others*

> **Chi:** *To enhance wisdom by broadening one's knowledge*
>
> **Shin:** *To be truthful at all times*
>
> **Tei:** *To care for the aged and those of humble station*

The *shoguns'* day seems like a distant mythic dream, afire with extreme ambitions and operatic passions. But how different are we, today, at the foundation of our humanity? Throughout time people evince nearly identical patterns in the ways we love, fight, anguish, and pursue our desires. We bear, raise, and worry for our children. We strive for success in a chosen craft and make great sacrifices, for better or worse, to secure our goals. The inevitability of death often influences our beliefs and intentions, much as we wrestle with questions of right and wrong, truth, identity, purpose, and survival.

But what can Bushido offer us today? How can its tough, formal standard of behavior possibly correlate to the fast-paced, technological, unpredictable course of modern life?

Consider the Samurai Way within its original framework. The Japanese feudal era framed a vast drama played out in political and military upheaval, radical new spiritual intensity, and a great flowering of cultural and artistic accomplishment. It can be tempting to reduce the Samurai legacy to its most obvious face values: the sensuality of royal courts, the heroics of physical combat, the pageantry of social transformation over five tumultuous centuries. However, beyond its directives on soldierly performance, the Samurai Code points again and again to the frailty and uncertainty of life. Stripped of its historical, and indeed its military contexts, the essence of Bushido is universal. Its most critical character is rooted in a vital sense of personal integrity and full presence in the moment.

Without its swords or its deadly martial tactics, the Samurai Way boils down to a basic human premise of building a strong ethical character. Bushido's bedrock of fortitude, kindness, honesty, and self-cultivation arguably contributed a unified ethical ballast for the stability of all Japanese society. Injustice, particularly toward the weak or underprivileged, was considered barbarous and inhumane. Loving compassion represented the highest virtue, expressed in a daily etiquette of sterling honesty and controlled public composure. Modest self-sacrifice for the common good was a paradigm for the finest human potential, and a benchmark for earnest emulation. Bushido identified these principles as distinctly soldierly aspirations; however, the code reflected fundamental Confucian teachings handed down for the more general purposes of a stable civil society for all.

With this in mind, perhaps Bushido's greatest relevance to contemporary life is seated in the principal virtue of honor, a binding and complete responsibility for one's actions, thoughts, feelings, and intentions. A true Samurai might define honor as a prudent balance between implied force and absolute mercy. The speed and intensity of our current social existence might well benefit from a genuine sense of honor and accountability to the greater good. Ultimately, our chances for a greater good must emanate first from building a culture that nourishes individual strength and vision, and the grit to respond judiciously to life's challenges. These civilized principles have an immediate and direct relevance to the modern mind. But without allegiance to an omnipotent feudal lord, what cause do we serve? And to whom are we obligated?

For the modern psyche, the Samurai's consummate discipline easily translates into unconditional surrender to a higher spiritual purpose. People still face the classic burning question of individual purpose within civilization.

Many of us urgently seek a specific role among the whole of humankind, through community, family, vocation, and visions of a peaceful, sustainable coexistence. This seeking process is elemental to our makeup as social beings. Centuries of endlessly shifting political tides, and the unstoppable flood of cultural and technological changes, have only reinforced the continuing relevance of these basic human motives and needs.

Perhaps the answer relates to the notion of a higher self, a deeply felt inner voice that governs our natural sense of responsibility and correct action—the voice that speaks a common language of compassion, decency, and abiding moral strength. None of these qualities necessarily comes easily or without sacrifice. But Bushido's primary rule entailed a fierce resolve to nurture these traits, and that resolve was considered a consequential reward in and of itself.

In most technologically advanced Western societies, we are no longer unified by binding submission to a master, or by a single spiritual or behavioral code. Over the past five centuries, the West has become flooded with rich, sometimes confusing cultural diversity and perplexing economic difficulties, causing us to confront questions that the Samurai never had to address.

In the twenty-first century, the delicate balance of our world has become even more precarious. The exacting velocity of daily existence leaves many people feeling exhausted, angry, and powerless. And many feel it's not enough to seek guidance from political, religious, or other public leadership alone. Our answers and questions must come from within—and through candid, meaningful discourse with peers and personal mentors. Perhaps we have entered a modern age of the *ronin*—the solitary Samurai, unbound from the restraints and comforts of a master, a government, or a retinue, unconditionally reliant upon his wits, his heart, and the internal mission to endless self-transformation.

That said, I have already mentioned the Samurai's premise of accountability to community and, beneath it, the powerful impulse to be part of something greater than the self alone. This desire for belonging is universal and not incompatible with the way of the ronin. It begins in the heart and extends into our actions. Reflecting on the Samurai Way brings us face-to-face with the question of our place in the world. This book attempts to link East and West with vital questions of purpose, belonging, and individual integrity. Look for yourself in these pages. Consider what you might have in common with the solitary ronin, unshakably secured to his path of truth seeking, self-knowledge, and the liberating tide of surrender.

名誉

THE WORD
OF A SAMURAI

*If a warrior makes loyalty and filial piety
one load, and courage and compassion
another, twenty-four hours a day
till his shoulders wear out—he'll be
a Samurai.*

—**Yamamoto Tsunetomo,**
from *Hagakure (Way of the Samurai)*

Bushi no ichi-gon translates to "the word of
a Samurai." In his regard for death and esteem
for life, the Samurai channeled his mental and
emotional clarity to enact the vow of truthfulness.

The warrior held an intractable distaste for petti-
ness, moral sloth, and above all, deceit. Cowardly
self-interest was seen as an unconscionable social
scourge, capable of generating mass instability and
encouraging individual susceptibility to evil.
Hence, the Samurai's conscription made him a
liable representative of justice and balanced rectitude. Community life around the Samurai was in
many ways dependent upon the warriors' public
example, which was meant to reflect the interests
of their feudal lords. People rightly viewed the
Samurai as guardians of a system that made their
daily lives possible and secure.

The immutable fact of death is the most
indispensable doctrine of Samurai culture. Beyond
their vow to welcome death in service to the
master, the Bushi were trained to reflect deeply on
the powerful emotions tied up with the eventuality
of death for all creatures. Their persistent meditation
on death was fittingly bound to a corresponding
veneration for life. Reverence for these existential

forces shored up the Samurai's single-minded approach to decisions that required swift, decisive action. His mindfulness of death rendered a foundation for acute self-examination, requiring him to confront the primal fears within his own consciousness. Through this tenacious inquiry, the Samurai grew to know himself and, in cultivating self-knowledge, to develop piercing mental clarity and a tensile emotional strength that would accommodate the unexpected and the unknown.

In the Samurai Way, all self-cultivation is geared to build a fearless, alert, self-aware personality, to meet life and death wholeheartedly, to be attentive to the truth that emerges in each moment, to recognize that change is the primal force beneath every event. And to stand alone with confidence in that solitude, while feeling connected to everything. Perhaps something like Bushido could have been created without words, like a silently transmitted body of pure military physics. But like all radical ideas, Bushido is anchored to words—language that shaped and animated the destiny of a subculture that is arguably accessible even today, wherever martial art is practiced. Its intrinsic value cannot, however, be limited to martial capacity. The utterances of Bushido resonate with the immediacy of any moment in time, under any conditions that test one's moral strength and purity of intent.

The poetic, arcane language of the Samurai Code itself draws one into a natural meditative dimension. Like *haiku* and Zen *koans*, its abstract imagery reveals lucid messages for individual interpretation. Its stark vernacular unearths a sophisticated spiritual essence beneath the raw warrior sensibility. Its plain yet mysterious phrases quickly penetrate the mind and puncture the very bottom of our most dearly held ego identifications. We become steeped in the moment, naked to the elements, and easily amenable to the rigorous zeal of Samurai consciousness. In the next chapter, "The Samurai Code," I present a number of Bushido affirmations and follow each with a subjective response. The voice I have used is deliberately free from reference to any particular place, people, or society. I have allowed each affirmation to guide the tone and mood of each response. Again, the language of Bushido compels the reader to absorb and define each message on a highly personal level. I hope my attempt prepares some small passage for the reader into untested territories in the struggle for self-knowledge, and perhaps a deeper awakening to the moment.

Self-knowledge, which the Western mind often deciphers in psychoanalytic terms, is for Bushido a morally driven process of introspection. With it arrives a challenge that is difficult to ignore and perhaps impossible to flee. The code is oddly compatible with today's contradictory Western mind. Perhaps Bushido's modern function is to engender a new Samurai mind that transcends cultural differences and rises to the universal vanishing point where all imagination is freed.

THE SAMURAI CODE

I have no parents; I make the Heavens and the Earth my Parents.

No matter how attached she remains to the bonds of her worldly clan, the Samurai soul truly belongs to the force of nature that creates all life. Solitary and exposed, the Samurai is rooted to the earth beneath her feet . . . and her vision is drawn from the wild expanse of heaven.

The Samurai responds to dual aspects of existence: her bloodline on earth and her primeval lineage in heaven. Family bloodline supplies her decency, values, and individual charm. It reinforces the simple goodness of passing a lifetime among loving kin who share a common and treasured past. Cosmic lineage suffuses the Samurai's destiny with risk and colors her life with the challenge to transcend ego, aspirations to luxury, a high social station, and a future of smoothly predictable events. It gives her a strange yet strangely familiar sense of belonging to something immeasurably vast, beyond her comprehension.

These two vines of familial belonging intertwine and sometimes ensnare the modern Samurai. She encounters herself in the snug hallways of her childhood home . . . and promptly loses herself in dreamy, remote stretches of territory with nothing more than chance beneath her feet. She struggles madly with reconciling her discordant family trees—till she awakens to perceive them as a single unruly fabric that traces the fluid design of her fate.

Eventually her Samurai temperament wins out, by surrendering to the blank slate that is every moment of life. Sometimes she gazes at it for hours, patiently waiting for a sign to act. When action comes, her mothers and fathers here and in heaven whip like fire through her brain and belly and heart.

In this mysterious familial way, she balances practical need with the astute correctness of deep insight. And in every act—at work, in the marketplace, in the secret longings of her heart— she honors her parentage well. She is the thread between the fertile soil of action and inspired celestial understanding.

I have no home;
I make the Tan T'ien my Home.

The *Tan T'ien* is the center of breath and balance in the body. It is located in the lower abdomen, just below the navel. Martial artists of all traditions are trained to focus their breath and consciousness in this area, to foster inward attention to their bodies and minds. This is also the case for some yoga and dance forms. Strong internal awareness enables the practitioner to become acutely alert to her or his external surroundings.

In Western parlance, we might call it "getting centered." For the Samurai, it is the only reliable place of refuge and stability. When familiar power structures fail, or when ordinary help is unavailable, the Tan T'ien offers the core inner security that is "home."

Getting centered is not an easy task. There is

so much noise in the world. Nearly all earthly desires distract from reaching a quiet internal focus. It takes will and, for those who choose it, some kind of trained discipline to generate the process. But even without training, without formal discipline, it is natural to seek and excavate the interior of one's real self.

All Samurai training is focused toward building the Tan T'ien. Beyond physical discipline, the abstract code itself impels the warrior to plunge unconditionally into the depths of mental and emotional inquiry. This inquiry is a basic exercise, not a fancy trick of the mind. When you look in the mirror, what manner of person do you see? Is it a face of integrity? Do the eyes speak the language of acceptance and compassion? Does the mouth form a real smile, or simply bare its teeth?

An honest, honorable face is usually worn by the person whose Tan T'ien is open wide with relaxed, unforced breathing. His inhale is smooth and regular, and spills easily to a fluid exhale without force. He wears the same face everywhere, with everyone he meets. Some days he is so centered that the Tan T'ien is doing all the work for him: answering the telephone, opening the mail, getting his children to school on time.

The Samurai is made of far more than mere martial prowess. He pursues the muted puzzle of his own humanity, no matter how taxing the journey. This is the true Way: to open up one's inner quest, hear its call, and trust its perfect sanctuary—without weapons, without regalia, without fealty to a master or slavery to a dogma. The Samurai just responds to what is needed, right now. This is also what Bushido means by "courage." Some days, it is all about finishing a dull chore, or apologizing to someone you have injured. These too are among the small acts that heal a piece of the world.

I have no divine power; I make
Honesty my Divine Power.

Truth is the bedrock of the Samurai's spiritual power. Knowing he has nothing to lose and everything to gain, he makes fearless honesty the medium of his fate. The world may disagree or even despise his candor—but he stands securely in the comfort of his firm integrity.

Stripped of the superficial social mask, the human spirit is instantly revealed as a vessel of pure honor. From this vessel pours the unvarnished truth, freed from triviality and false good humor. A modern Samurai is impatient with people who avoid revealing their sincere thoughts and feelings. He is even more critical of his own inadequacies— when his truth is spoken too harshly for no particular reason, or too lightly to be taken with fitting seriousness.

The Samurai's Honesty marks his place in the world. His Divine Power touches events with the rare grace of unembroidered sincerity. He is grounded in his truth. He brings it into the boardroom, into the bedroom, to his morning reflection in the mirror. His hindsight is clear and informs his foresight that he will have no regrets as an old man. This too prepares the Samurai for an effortless surrender to death, whenever it might come.

I have no eyes; I make
the Flash of Lightning my Eyes.

The Samurai's magnetic presence cannot be ignored. She is pure contained ferocity, the force of nature incarnate. The necessity of the moment is all she sees. And, through the evidence of her actions, others perceive the intensity and integrity of her inmost vision.

And what is vision, after all, but a living connection with the elemental power of inspiration? Like lightning, it can appear to descend from an external phenomenon—something encountered in the world that reaches out and shakes up the creative essence inside a human being. The source can be turbulent as a monsoon, or silent as a patch of night sky. Everything that exists holds this matchless promise of inspiration.

But inspiration needs a human vessel to

become realized. It demands the penetrating eyes and ears of a Samurai, so absorbed in life that she is a constant vehicle for creative potential. By normal standards, the risk is high. She must learn to manage the vertiginous heights and humbling lows that constitute a vividly held existence.

The Samurai view of the world is raw as lightning, touched with inherent qualities of illumination and the passionate heat of action. Over time, her other soldierly virtues unfold and help to balance and internalize these intoxicating energies. She tempers her high-strung nature with gratitude for the simple beauties of the day: taking quiet solace in the shadows on a fence, or drinking in the colors of her careworn laundry. Or learning to steady her elation by spending an honorable hour at the kitchen sink, slicing fruits for savoring later on, knowing the thrill of silence when she would otherwise speak.

I have no ears;
I make Sensibility my Ears.

How does the Samurai listen? From the heart, to feel what is being felt. From the bones, to move in the rhythm of what's happening in each moment. From the very bloodstream, to let right action flow from what's truly needed now.

The Samurai hears the real message beneath mere words, and sees the truth beneath mere gesture. In business, her ears receive hidden signals under the banal mechanics of negotiation. In love, she quietly opens to receive what's being offered and asked. In spirit, she draws incentive and solace from listening to the beloved with every part of her being. People entrust her with their secrets, because she has less to say and more to hear.

The happy discipline of listening clears the

mind of excess noise. The Samurai places herself squarely in the moment and opens shrouded channels to the inner voice that guides appropriate, righteous action. She listens and is led by the music of her heart, where real answers surface above the dissonance of worldly distractions.

The Samurai trusts Sensibility. She quiets the noise of insecurity and doubt. She listens from the foundation of her being, where ego steps aside to let truth emerge intact. She stops everything, and hears the music of awareness in her smallest, most hidden act.

I have no means;
I make Docility my Means.

Bushi no nasake, "the tenderness of the warrior,"
is the indispensable balancing attribute of all
masterly fighters. Samurai composure is expressed
in civility, kindness, and genuine concern for
others, particularly those who are vulnerable or
oppressed. At its core, Docility is the means to a
greater awareness of what action is needed at the
moment—or whether action is appropriate at all.
Appropriate decisions cannot be made by a mind
that is fraught with the heat of excess passion.

Docility is a uniquely subtle discipline. It is
the practice of conserving one's vital energies to
create a rich reserve of internal power. The
seasoned Samurai does not squander his vigor on
petty emotions. His inner resources are carefully
withheld for the moment when serious need arises.

The Samurai's undisturbed countenance generates a quiet, reasonable atmosphere around him. His gentle chivalry enables easy communication under stressful circumstances. Mildness only enhances the Samurai's charisma and magnetism. People are charmed and intrigued by this humane junction of elegant comportment and contained internal power. The warrior gracefully sets the mood for clear negotiation and mutually favorable results. When he rises to achieve a goal, the Samurai's lucid, focused ardor can move others to uphold his cause.

Docility means allowing your wife to scowl because you forgot to buy milk—and then apologizing, even if you do not feel bad about your forgetfulness. Docility is quietly making up the difference, being bigger than a petty conflict, letting go of trivial injury when friendship is at stake. Knowing when and when not to react with action, or meet a fragile moment with gentle silence, receptive as sand to water.

*I have no magic power; I make
Personality my Magic Power.*

The Samurai is acutely conscious of human dynamics. She knows that events turn on the personalities of those involved in any situation— and that each personality brings new chemistry to the mix.

All of us come to the table with individual agendas. It can take a long time of sifting through the social masks that people present to get a true picture of their intentions. We are all masters of hiding who we are in order to leverage a position in life. We are all actors, behaving as we imagine others expect to secure our place in the order of things. Personality as we know of it is a grab bag of facial expressions, stitched up with predictable words we think everyone wants to hear. Most of us are trained to build a personality that will somehow get us what we want, however great or humble our desires.

Part of this "training" is the honing of a personality that we present to the world, so that others might see us as unique or, at the very least, unthreatening. Relationships are often built upon the illusion of personalities that are mere shadows of who we really are. People rarely know one another at a level deeper than their shadow selves. This is why so many relationships dissolve over sudden, insignificant events. There can be no substance of truth between masks or shadows.

So what is this "magic power" of Personality? And how does the Samurai employ it to achieve her aim? Is it the same old game, played the way we are taught to play?

It is simple: The Samurai does not script her actions according to her own, or others', conventional expectations. She releases her natural eloquence in the plainest of terms. Her eyes speak for her mouth, her mouth speaks for her heart.

Her mind is present, attentive, in tune with her ethical integrity. She does not manipulate with words. Whatever she needs to say flows from unaffected sincerity and simple self-knowledge. This is genuine Personality, unblemished by greed, fear, or opportunism.

A Samurai's Magic Power is the unforced charisma of a person without guile. This kind of person honors daily life by serving as an integral part of it. Her presence alone exposes fakery and posturing, which are more like sorcery than magic. She knows that magic flows naturally through anyone who does not build their own impediments to truth.

I have no body;
I make Stoicism my Body.

Maintaining a firm, stoic mentality frees the Samurai from attachment to physical luxury. He can enjoy a lavish feast in an opulent palace while caring nothing for its allure. Self-possessed, indifferent to worldly entrapments, the Samurai owes nothing to anyone but for allegiance to his code.

Today we are surrounded by greater and greater temptations to extravagance. This is not a bad thing in and of itself. But it takes resolute detachment to enjoy luxury with awareness while not becoming its sleepy captive. Entitlement to opulence is a seductive trap. It is not unusual for people to break down over the loss of material wealth. If a person's identity crashes along with his bank account, he has a great opportunity to find out who he really is and what he really values.

Living in wealth or comfort is not the problem. The problem lies in having a personal identification with wealth, or with the power to gain and hold it, or with temporal power itself.

No matter how great or how meager his estate, the Samurai's appreciation for comfort is colored by a healthy disregard for excess. His master is self-awareness. It keeps his priorities in balance, and holds him to the keen knowledge of worldly impermanence. But the rich person must regularly take his own vital signs. Like his friend the Zen monk, the Samurai is bound to a vow of poverty. The Samurai can have money but does not think that he *is* money. The Samurai can eat rich food, wear fine clothing, or live in a fine house. But he is free from illusion about the intrinsic value of these things. He must be detached enough to disown anything that threatens his clarity of purpose or sense of true self. If he waits till wealth is taken from him by misfortune or by death, he will not experience the quiet satisfaction of walking away from it on his own.

I have no designs; I make Seizing Opportunity by the Forelock my Design.

To remain wakeful and spontaneous, the Samurai keeps her mind empty of schemes. Her ready, instinctive response to the moment takes precedence over preconceived strategies and designs. She does not plot, plan, or jockey for position or favors. And this is her formula for success.

How can this be? Without a game plan, how can the Samurai make effective use of her mind and talents? How can she know when to draw her sword, keep it sheathed, or venture nakedly into the moment?

It comes down to practical spontaneity. Each phase of a circumstance has a life of its own. And no matter how prudently one might contrive an outcome, things keep changing anyway. By staying in the moment, the Samurai does not lose herself in a tangle of strategies. She remains in touch with what needs to be done now. She knows that every moment is just one bead on an endless strand of events—and that events gain momentum to produce a climax. This process guides the timing and the nature of her actions.

Seizing Opportunity is the art of patient impatience. The Samurai waits for a sliver of chance to open. It is most likely to occur in the least obvious place, so patience is essential. Beneath the waiting, impatience simmers quietly, ready to spark a decisive leap into action. This all sounds very dramatic. But it is in fact a thing of great subtlety. If we are honest with ourselves (and with one another), the most urgent tasks before us are about relationship. People are continually sending signals to each other, but most of the time we're too preoccupied with ourselves to receive those messages, much less relate properly to the messenger. If we lack awareness of another person's state, how can we know what actions to take, and when? How much time we waste, how many opportunities are lost!

The Samurai mother watches her child at play, to see what he is seeing and better understand him. Is it a moment for him alone? Should she step into his reverie? If so, when? The same acuity guides her through a difficult business meeting, a high-pressure interview, or a friendly game of poker. She takes in little gestures, facial expressions, body language, changes in vocal tone. She is engaged in the details and misses very little. It is all so interesting, so instructive, so beautiful. By simply paying attention, she knows when to act, when to speak, when to be silent, when to stay, and when to take her leave.

I have no miracles; I make
Righteous Laws my Miracle.

The Samurai is wired for action. He neither claims to manifest miracles nor looks to heaven to provide them. He is a realist. It is against his character to expect miracles from something he cannot see, feel, or sense in the world around him. He wisely leaves celestial miracles to priests, saints, and magicians.

Instead, the Samurai's Miracle is a direct response to an urgent need in the present moment. Within him lies the clarity to perceive what is happening beneath the surface of events, and, when action is needed, make a proper move to rectify the situation. His action neither indulges a momentary whim nor unleashes a selfish emotional reaction. To act with integrity, he relies on knowledge of self and of human nature. He is supported from within by an understanding of Righteous Laws that create balance where there is inequity and order where there is chaos.

Righteous Laws create a framework that allows miracles to manifest naturally. They exist in concert with the cosmic laws that embrace every vow in the Samurai Code. Where there is wrongdoing, the Samurai performs the miracle of rectitude. Where there is hardship, he enacts the miracle of courage. Witness of suffering calls him to embody benevolence. Roughness and vulgarity rouse him to politeness. He meets cowardice and fraud with authenticity and veracity. His honor dissolves ignorance and elevates dignity. His loyalty is the antidote to betrayal.

The Samurai knows the miracle of commitment to friends, to family, to a beloved cause; the miracle of tenderness toward all living things; the miracle of humble apology when it's due; the miracle of rocking his infant child through a colicky night. He knows the miracle of liking himself, with or without outside affirmation, and the miracle of changing just one small thing for the betterment of someone else.

Most of these miracles go unseen, unsung, undocumented. They are the miracles of a life driven by a higher intelligence of the soul reaching for enlightenment.

I have no principles; I make Adaptability to all Circumstances my Principle.

Rigidity cannot masquerade as principle. Beneath its formal pledge, Bushido is fluid as a summer stream, sweetening the creative flow and bathing the warrior in cool awareness. Firmly grounded in integrity, the Samurai must yield to circumstance as a fern responds to morning dew. Like water wearing away river stones, adaptability erodes fear and releases the wonderment of innocent awareness. From this purity of mind, principle can ideally shape itself in harmony with the moment at hand.

But new circumstances are a tricky portal to the unknown. To enter unfamiliar turf with confidence, the Samurai cannot be enslaved to preconceived ideas of right and wrong. She must bend to the facts as they are presented in the here and now. And even for great Samurai, a strange predicament may be loaded with terrifying uncertainty and isolation.

This dilemma underscores the Samurai's vow to endure loneliness with grace. She must go within and gather resources to find fresh answers and suitable actions. To banish her doubts, she must uncover new reservoirs of flexibility. The process can be painful. Her instincts may contradict the successful results of past experience. She might wrestle with fear of public reaction to her unusual choices. But the challenge compels her to innovate, tap untested skills, and deepen her trust in the unknown.

Adaptability is the fountain of youth and the tutor of wisdom. It exposes the Samurai's own resistance to change, and calls her to end old patterns that don't serve the moment. The freer she becomes, the more attuned she is to the world with all its fleeting sparks of vitality. She uncoils, loosens, pours her being into the hidden nuances of life— and proceeds unhindered into fair, truthful, and relevant action.

*I have no tactics; I make
Emptiness and Fullness my Tactics.*

Tactical psychology is the prerogative of politicians and merchants. They hold no interest for the Bushi. He has neither the time nor the luxury for an agenda beyond the exigencies of the moment. Though skilled in the strategies of his craft, he nonetheless operates from a stance of readiness for unexpected change—usually in the inevitable monkey wrench flung into his best-laid plans.

The Samurai is empty as a fountain base built to receive a continuous water supply. He uses Emptiness to manage the flow of new information that defies the logic of his game plan. His ego is swept bare, disengaged from jockeying for power. He sits still and listens. In doing so, he transforms mere information into genuine, usable knowledge. And knowledge feeds his courage for a bold response to unanticipated trouble. The Bushi is thus freed to invent, to experiment, to embrace other opinions that will enlighten his intent and guide his actions.

Emptiness is the flip side of a vast spiritual Fullness. This balance is essential to the Samurai's wholeness. He is fertile with an abundance of honor, humility, and unselfish commitment to the common good. His Fullness of heart embraces the dignity of every living thing. He's unconcerned with receiving praise yet finds nobility in the simplest expressions of daily life.

The Samurai's overflow of human experience precludes any need for the tactics of scheming self-interest. His reward is the empty Fullness that carries no burden of future gain. His fountain empties and fills at once, replenished in ecstatic surrender to the moment.

I have no talent; I make
Ready Wit my Talent.

Playing court jester is a welcome relief from momentary tension. It is easier and healthier than making a display of talent for its own sake, or for the sake of currying favor with others. The Samurai has no need for unctuous adulation. His talents are kept in modest reserve, percolating quietly for the moment they will be needed at full throttle.

Ready Wit is the Samurai's genius for replacing tension with evanescent goodwill. The practice of Ready Wit must embody precisely what it states— a gift for quick, incisive speech that is immediately available to the astute Bushi. His humor is finely tuned to human interplay and the flow of emotions within a group. Never mean-spirited, Samurai humor is nonetheless characterized by an artful nod to the absurd. The warrior's cognizance of injustice and the certainty of death doubtless infuse his strong inclination to irony, and throws his own vulnerable lot in with that of his fellow human beings.

At times, Samurai wit is a necessary means of successful negotiation. One dose of self-possessed drollery can pierce awkward moments with the speed and keenness of a shogun's foil. A well-placed, elegantly crafted remark can tip the balance of conversation from coy concealment to forthright transparency or from edgy provocation to civilized candor. (On more than one ancient occasion, this highly prized conversational skill may have prevented a tipsy Samurai from slicing another in half.)

Modern writers and linguists have expressed dismay at the apparent decline in the art of discourse. Today's Samurai must find apt moments for the injection of whip-smart, utterly relevant wit, laced with eccentric wisdom and self-deprecating truth.

*I have no friends; I make
my Mind my Friend.*

Loneliness is a prevailing condition of people everywhere. For the Samurai, loneliness is the key to grasping the fragility of his own existence, bound up with the temporal nature of all life.

Historically, tolerating loneliness was imperative to the warrior's life of extremes in physical hardship, martial jeopardy, and severe self-examination. Even if the Samurai was a beloved family man and respected member of his retinue and local community, he remained mindful of the sudden, often calamitous, changes that can isolate and crush the human spirit. The Bushido-trained soldier practiced the excruciating art of facing life as if he was irretrievably removed from the apparent mirage of basic social comfort.

However strictly he interpreted the way of

loneliness, the Samurai was paradoxically linked to his fellow humans through the vows he adopted—kindness, compassion, and love of his soldierly peers and countrymen. These qualities cannot be expressed under pretense. And the Bushido creed abhorred superficial, inauthentic behaviors. His pact with truly human feelings forced the Samurai to be deeply engaged with people while setting himself apart existentially.

Considering this painful, self-imposed paradox, it follows that the Samurai must indeed befriend his own mind. He must nurture an increasingly supple balance between his acceptance of loneliness and his natural disposition to giving and receiving personal love. This is especially true for the modern Samurai, whose social context is not embedded in the brotherhood of an imperial retinue or an inflexibly patriarchal social climate. We are also blessed with the pleasing influences of greater gender equality and freer interaction between the sexes.

Still, there is a timeless and universal intelligence behind the concept of befriending one's own mind. The notion implies a serious obligation to care and feed our most precious asset—the experience of living consciousness, and its potential to lead us to the gift of our own evolving humanity.

The modern Samurai has received the gift of time and evolution. It frees him to cultivate a higher self in the intimate, trusting company of other like-minded, like-passioned creatures— family, lovers, teachers, newborn babies, and yes, welcome friends all.

I have no enemy; I make
Incautiousness my Enemy.

Bushido trains the soldier's mind in the artistry
of caution. Life and death, failure and triumph,
honor and shame are all hinged upon the Samurai's
aptitude for vigilance. In view of such distressing
stakes, it is no wonder that Incautiousness is the
Samurai's sole enemy.

Caution is not remotely akin to the pathology
of paranoia. It is, rather, another extension of the
Samurai's lifelong cultivation of total awareness.
She must nurture many subtle skills to amplify
this awareness. Her success is reliant on a
confluence of discretion, prudence, heedfulness,
and circumspection. By unifying these qualities,
she opens up to a surprising range of understated
sensitivities. (Great Samurai have been said to
hear the breath of a butterfly on a window. Even

if it's a fable, this is a sublime degree of awareness to aspire to.)

The contemporary Samurai may or may not be called upon to employ the art of caution on a traditional battlefield. But there is no question she will find vast use for it in every phase of daily life. Like calligraphy and tea ceremony, the Samurai Code is a weave of interlocking disciplines. Caution is a sister to listening, just as Docility is linked to Emptiness and Fullness. In truth, they are interconnected and interdependent, manifesting one crucial and abiding end: the evolution of pure consciousness, for which the Samurai lives and breathes.

I have no armor; I make
Benevolence my Armor.

The Samurai feels no need for protection. His surrender to the certainty of death renders fear of potential danger a questionable concern at best. *I have no armor.* He tells us in an offhand, unembellished way that he is, to all practical purposes, defenseless. Then, *I make Benevolence my Armor.* What manner of soldier is this?

Clearly, the Samurai is not speaking the language of a physical battlefield. His unconcern for safety passes like vapor through the obvious reference to armor and pierces the very soul of Bushido. In other words, the warrior with a heart of stone is no Samurai.

Benevolence is the ultimate outcome of total awareness. The Samurai struggles for years to strip his senses of noise and turn his thoughts from pointless diversion. He trains his body with the severity of a gladiator. His mind is whipped into shape by every temporal experience that leads him back to the source—Bushido. And Bushido is, in the end, a training manual for a unique evolution of the psyche.

Benevolence is the condition to which every Samurai aspires. And the effort is daunting. It's easy to slip through the cracks and simply achieve mental dexterity and decent manners. These qualities will get the basic job done, whether he's defending a point of honor, a way of life, or straddling the frontiers of business success and social acceptance. Any of these might make him a soldier, or even a "master of the universe." But they do not make him a Samurai.

The Samurai is both plagued and blessed with a passionate urgency to be liberated from himself. He chooses Bushido because it relentlessly holds up a mirror to his inmost fears and insecurities. And his cause is to build a fully awake, glad, and just human being. Even if he fails, he succeeds. His intention is stainless and perfect in itself.

I have no castle; I make
Immovable Mind my Castle.

The Samurai's old friend, her mind, has now become Immovable Mind. There is no need for the battlements and moat of a castle. The Samurai surrounds Mind with the precious fortification of the spirit. She is thus at liberty to strike out with confidence into the most hostile districts, with no worry for her safety, and again, with no visible armor.

Immovable Mind has a great deal in common with Benevolence. The Samurai needs no castle because she has learned to traverse the most fearful realms of her own being. She meditates on the brevity of life. She is accustomed now to the noise and mess of becoming more human. Part of her hears only the distant cries of her past anguish; and the mess more resembles Proust's madeleine, a small but knowing fragment of a grander, more significant story.

Immovable Mind is tested at every turn. It even seems to delight in making the bold Samurai shiver with discontent. But eventually the warrior gathers her might—from Heaven and Earth, from Righteous Laws, Adaptability, Ready Wit—and sits in stillness, listening to the silent castle of her heart.

Immovable Mind is the Samurai's towering strength. A humble strength, steadily built of mud and toil, of surrender to life and its panoply of circumstance.

I have no sword; I make
No Mind my Sword.

With empty hands, the Samurai steps into his final sanctuary. All he hears is the sound of everything, in one seamless chorus. It whistles like a teakettle, like wind, like a very old forest at night. He can hear himself somewhere in there, too, like a familiar creak in a porch swing rocker. It makes him smile a little.

No Mind lifts him out of the world and roots him precisely within it. There is nothing to fight, defend, or charge.

If he had to, or wanted to, he could.

No Mind neither welcomes nor evades death. It no longer meditates on death's actuality, or its imminent arrival. There is no busy self here to invest a moment in the idea of death anyway. No

Mind is just another point of entry to Bushido, which leads again to No Mind.

What is a sword? Who cares to wield it? In whose name, and for what reward? Is it for the child pushing a ridge of gravel in the rain, imposing his tiny Samurai will on whatever is within reach? Is it for the old man in a crumpled hat, making his way to morning coffee and the company of his favorite waitress? For the thousands who press down subway stairs as if they were one seamless chorus of intention, task, and worry?

I have no sword. No Mind is not even my sword anymore. Bushido stories flood past my No Mind, my once immovable mind that moves now like a wind-tossed newspaper clinging to a bough. Out of nowhere and nothingness, I sit at last in the ruins of my earthly bounds.

WHO IS A SAMURAI?

A Samurai is naked as a broodmare. As raw as the wind. Relentless as the sea. Plain as summer rain. Alight with purpose. Unequivocally awake. Flooded with receptivity. Empty as an open palm.

A true Samurai has little patience for her own shortcomings. The blade of consciousness is milled against the grain of her nature. It sharpens her thirst for growth. She will do whatever is necessary to reveal, and be revealed, in the never-ending present.

The true Samurai is a bottomless pool of pure potential. He is possibility itself. He is nothingness. Made more of reserve than action, more of action than speech.

The Samurai is touched by a divine lunacy.

She welcomes the absurdities of life—the peculiar magnetism of change, the impermanence of resolution, the inevitability of death.

The true Samurai: if a still pond would speak.

A BUSHIDO
TIME LINE

*Which is worse—to err in matters
concerning the ranks of men, or to stray
from the Way of the Samurai?*

—Nabeshima Tadanao, age fifteen, quoted in
  Hagakure by Yamamoto Tsunetomo

Had I not known
that I was dead
already
I would have mourned
my loss of life.

—Death poem of Ota Dokan, 1486

The Bushido cult etched indelible traces on every feature of Japanese civilization. Its tenets shaped a gentry class of warrior akin to the medieval knights of Europe, whose impact similarly enriched Western art, literature, music, and social constructs and behaviors. The comparison is also politically apt. Both the Samurai and their European counterparts were products of their respective feudal societies. Beyond the indisputably contrary orientations of East and West, each of these military models was indentured to strict codes of self-sacrifice, justice, honor, discipline and excellence, personal refinement, and undivided loyalty to one's master. Their legacies shaped the political outcomes and cultural identities of their peoples and fuel the imaginations of modern minds everywhere.

Late in the eighth century, a protracted struggle ensued among Japanese property masters who sought to protect their holdings and, later, to extend individual control into neighboring districts. These *daimyo*, or warlords, ruled regional provinces under the emperor and vied for the title of *shogun*—the richest, most powerful sovereign in the country and nearest influence to the imperial throne. Such intense rivalries called for the use of military force at an unprecedented level. The Samurai, unconditionally devoted to the service and protection of their lords, were assembled as the enabling instruments in what became a seven-hundred-year contest of wills in the struggle to rule Japan.

Early Samurai (originally "*saburai*") were seeded from pre-Heian imperial guards, conscripted foot soldiers, and rough, uneducated mercenaries. They were hired by feudal landowners who sought to seize control of Honshu, Japan's main island in the eighth and ninth centuries. Each Samurai was one of a retinue maintained by a particular provincial lord. Living by a cult of the sword, early Bushi troops worshipped athletic prowess and martial skill. Fierce loyalty to their masters and a binding fearlessness of death vaunted their deserved reputation as formidable adversaries. Over time, elaborate battle suits, fearsome masks, and sophisticated weaponry furthered the Samurai legend among subjects of the territories. State-of-the-art double-edged sabers, capable of cleaving a man in two, certainly did little to inhibit the growing national prestige of Bushi culture.

By the twelfth century, these superbly trained fighters were highly visible, eminently influential members of the Japanese aristocracy. At the top levels of the military power structure, the Bushi were awarded many privileges, including generous stipends, the right to travel freely throughout the country, and permission to wear the long and short swords signifying their elevated social rank.

The military system was built upon a hierarchy of status within a given retinue, based on one's performance in every soldierly art. The pinnacle of Samurai greatness has been famously modeled on the number of heads a soldier could lay before his master's feet. But rank promotions were often clinched by a subtler ideal of meritocracy: that is, a soldier's wisdom in the application of his craft, demonstrated by a strong personal integrity built upon Bushido's fastidious code. This amalgam of individual responsibility and highly codified behavior was expanded and refined by successive Bushi generations.

Heian Period (794–1185)

The Samurai began their long tenure as private mercenaries. The Bushi culture became an indispensable commodity to landowners protecting their properties. Near the close of the Heian Period, two military clans, the Minamoto and Taira families, vied for control over the country and further expanded their warrior regiments.

Kamakura Period (1192–1333)

In 1185, the Minamoto family succeeded in its quest for supremacy. In 1192, Minamoto Yoritomo founded a militia government in Kamakura, and serving as its highest officer—shogun—he became the de facto ruler of Japan.

Muromachi Period (1333–1573)

Between 1467 and 1573, Japan was plunged into sustained conflict among dozens of independent states. The demand for Samurai escalated. Between the turf wars, Samurai often took work as farmhands.

Azuchi-Momoyama Period (1573–1603)

Toyotomi Hideyoshi was the legendary shogun who reunified Japan. Infamous for his introduction of a harsh social caste system, Hideyoshi is also known as the vitriolic student of Rikyu, founder of tea ceremony (*chanoyu*). Hideyoshi compelled all Samurai to choose between farm work and military conscription.

Edo Period (1603–1868)

During the Edo Period, the Samurai stood at the pinnacle of the caste order, followed by farmers, artisans, and merchants. There was minor opposition to the strict caste rules for Samurai, led by the Ronin class of masterless warriors.

Tokugawa Ieyasu eliminated one last rival, and for 250 years a relative peace prevailed in Japan. Peacetime eroded the shoguns' need for Samurai, and most remaining warriors became bureaucrats, teachers, or artists. In 1868 the feudal period ended, and with it the Samurai class.

The code was eventually consolidated in writing through three seminal volumes, *A Book of Five Rings*, the sixteenth-century strategic guide to Kendo (*Way of the Sword*) by Miyamoto Musashi; the *Bushido Shoshinsu*, which documents the deeds of eminent shoguns such as Toyotomi Hideyoshi; and *Hagakure* by Yamamoto Tsunetomo, published in 1716 when the Samurai subculture had begun to show signs of decline in morale. These texts are largely anecdotal and aphoristic. They are meant to teach by example. To the Western psyche, the single-minded Bushi can appear an eccentric lot. Much of the code seems unutterably opaque. Its logic and etiquette were conceived for a wholly engrossed cult of fighters, men deliberately estranged from the maze of quotidian distractions. Bushido expression stood worlds apart from the vernacular of more moderate worldly exertions. The warrior code remained a canon unto itself until the pivotal years of the early twelfth century, when the Samurai discovered their striking affinity with Zen Buddhism.

The essence of early Samurai thought and conduct was informed by Chinese spiritual philosophies. Strict Confucian tenets injected teachings into Bushido life that governed practical relationships within the social world, the political environment, and above all, family. The Samurai were schooled to become living examples of Confucian-inspired hierarchies among their family members, social classes, and political structures. Bushido's code of public conduct was, in part, intended to model Confucian ideology through the warrior's daily life in his community. Devotion to one's blood relations supplied an ethical mooring for the Samurai's vow of compassion. His pledge to look after family members included a general obligation to others outside his clan— those who were weaker, less fortunate, and in need of protection. Hence, the "extended family" in a Samurai's village, town, or city were as important to protect as members of his own clan.

While Confucian dogma held dominant authority over worldly matters, Shinto exerted the sway of cosmic accountability. Based in ancestor worship, Shinto affirmed the imperial family bloodline as the primal origin of Japan, endowing the emperor with a divine nature as the embodiment of heaven on earth. Shinto also teaches that the earth not only serves human needs but is also the sacred dwelling of the gods and all the nation's forefathers. These cardinal beliefs invigorated the Samurai's fervent allegiance to country and his unequivocal devotion to his master.

Between his job requirements, social responsibilities, and religious obligations, the Samurai's existence was a grid of highly visible, tightly interlaced covenants, all functioning under the implicit duress of life-and-death consequences for the warrior, for his master, and for the good of Japan as a whole.

From the early twelfth through the late sixteenth century, Samurai philosophy and conduct were further shaped by Zen Buddhism. Although the practice of Zen was imported from China by Japanese scholar-monks as early as the mid-seventh century, it did not fully take root until late in the twelfth century. In fact, in 845, Zen was outlawed in Japan, a casualty of the country's ongoing political strife and of Zen's inherently radical contradictions to the conservative nature of Confucianism. Some three centuries later, the new religion would exercise a quick and permanent impact on the Bushi, who by then had unknowingly paved the way for Zen's return to Japan with a revolution of their own.

For two hundred years the Taira and Minamoto clans grappled in a protracted bid for supremacy and, through the twelfth century, engaged in continuous conflict marked by palace coups, power-sharing deals, temple wars, shrine cults, dramatic suicides, and the near decimation of the Taira clan in one vicious battle. The militant fervor of this era was evidenced in the participation of innumerable women from civil society who felt compelled to fight on behalf of their clans and courts. (However, few women were recognized by the Samurai as true soldiers. Among them was Tomoe Gozen, attached to the court of Kiso Yoshinaka, a warlord aligned with the Minamoto, who set upon the standing Taira clan in the 1180s. Tomoe's elegant style in archery and sword craft and her ferocity on the battlefield were rivaled only by her delicate beauty.)

The closing decades of the twelfth century issued the most critical and lasting turning point for the Samurai class as a whole. The imperial nobility had progressively weakened, while the warrior clans had grown stronger. Control of the empire was eventually seized by Minamoto Yoritomo, who overthrew the imperial seat and instituted the Samurai government in Kamakura. With this unprecedented conquest, the military classes, previously regarded with a combination of fear and condescension for their lack of classical education, completely supplanted the de facto sovereignty of the imperial house and the nobility. For the next two hundred and fifty years, Japan would experience its first sustained period of peace and political stability.

名誉

Epilogue

ZEN AND THE ART OF WAR

A monk cannot fulfill the Buddhist Way if he doesn't manifest compassion without, and store up courage within. And if a warrior does not manifest courage externally, and hold enough compassion within his heart to burst his chest, he cannot become a retainer. Ergo, the monk uses the warrior as his model for courage, and the warrior pursues the compassion of a monk.

—Tannen, seventeenth-century Zen priest and Tsunetomo's teacher

Zen in ninth-century Japan germinated in concert with the throes of vicious warlord conflicts, and alongside the emergence of groundbreaking art forms such as *tanka*, which set the standard for classical Japanese poetry. The country's courtship with Zen had begun as early as the seventh century, with Japanese emissaries visiting China to study with Zen monks, and ended abruptly in 845 with an imperial injunction against the religion in Japan.

Zen received new official sanction in 1192, when a dynamic, charismatic young Japanese seeker named Eisai, who had spent over twenty years studying Buddhism in China, returned home to establish Rinzai, a particularly strict sect of Zen. Eisai's timing was beyond reproach: Japan had arrived at a historic crossroads, and with the Samurai government in place, the national mind, and particularly the new ruling class, was ripe for revolutionary ideas.

While military governors continued the inherited custom of intimate transactions between state and religious leadership, it was nonetheless plainly time for a change. Tendai and Shingon, Buddhist forms that had reached Japan three centuries earlier, did not resonate for the warrior. These sects were too complex in form, too conceptually rarified for the stripped-down rigors of Bushi mentality. But Zen, with its immediacy and directness, was the perfect spiritual match for the Samurai. With the founding of Rinzai and, soon after, the first monastery dedicated to Zen as an independent sect, the absorption of Zen philosophy heralded a religious and cultural sea change that would leave its imprint for centuries to come.

The Zen resurgence was a fin-de-siècle phenomenon. It unfolded in a time of passionate martial spirit throughout Japan. In the eleventh century, there had even been clashes between temples that were loyal to different warlords; a significant number of Buddhist priests were trained in the combat arts. By the thirteenth century, Zen monks and Samurai warriors discovered the parity in their disciplines. Their kinship pivoted on moral affinities—courage, compassion, honesty, poverty—and attaining a state of full presence in the moment. Like Bushido, Zen was, to a degree, built upon a spiritual covenant with the certain reality of death. Zen teachings were also infused with compatible elements of Confucian wisdom, which had molded Samurai consciousness for two centuries. This fusion of complementary philosophies doubtless made instant sense to the Samurai and gave them a quick grasp of Zen sensibility.

As representatives of a standing military government, the Samurai were at a crucial phase of potential growth. Monastic life, an intriguing admixture of quiet order and industrious activity, spoke volumes to the Bushi. Rinzai's formal severity doubtless appealed to the Samurai sense

of order and stringency. The Samurai recognized
Zen, and its practice of classical art forms, as
an instrument for deepening self-knowledge
outside military life. Zen philosophy strongly
inferred the prospect of balancing external valor
with mercy and serenity—a Confucian ideal that
was familiar to Bushido adherents. Above all, the
Samurai saw in Zen a vivid reflection of Bushido's
charge to cultivate a still, clear, focused mind
that was impervious to fear of death. To this end,
Zen supplied the most practical path for a
warrior's enlightenment.

The monks also inspired the Samurai to blend
soldierly discipline with a fertile refinement of mind
and spirit through poetry, painting, calligraphy, tea
ceremony, and meditation. Individual Japanese art
forms, conceptually interwoven, also express the
integral connection between human beings and
nature. Making a simple tea bowl from clay, or
swiping an energetic flow of ink across a page,
surely infused a celebratory, even humorous,

dimension to the Samurai's bidden respect for life.
The monastery was a spiritual incubator, where
soldierly stoicism was integrated with emotional
calm, self-mastery in the thick of chaos, and a
profound grasp of temporal existence. Zen's
creative milieu, and its unworried sense of the
absurd, freed the Samurai to investigate more
sensitive facets of their humanity, which in turn
nourished the resolute vigor of the warrior mind.

The benefits of this odd fraternity were
thoroughly reciprocal. Theirs was a near-predictable
encounter between two breeds of restless seekers.
Zen monks beheld a worldly counterpart in the
warrior persona. Their insular monastic ways
were pleasantly shaken by the advent of the
Samurai. Soldiers brought the harsher facts of life
to the monks' doors. At a level of deep practice,
monks were challenged to conflate their vow of
compassion for all sentient beings with the
Samurai's boldness to face all of life.

Knowledge of the sutras and sitting zazen

had always shared equal berth with the Zen monks'
pledge to embrace everything as a manifestation
of the Buddha. The tough, unpolished warriors
were a perfect test of that pledge. Beneath their
intimidating armor, they were childlike sponges
for everything that Zen offered. The soldiers
wanted it all, from the essential temple teachings
through the sensitivities of tea ceremony etiquette
to the subtle motion of grinding a block of
calligraphy ink. And their Zen mentors hungered
to know the soldiers' constancy of devotion—and
the raw courage to defend that devotion at any
cost, especially that of one's own life. Perhaps
their lessons from the Samurai have been most
acutely fixed in modern memory by the
motionless monks who immolated themselves to
protest war. In a perfect union of Bushido and
Sutra, these martyrs brought the warriors' code
into practice as messengers of peace.

The fellowship between monk and warrior
produced a wave of ethical dialogue that touched

the core of both Zen and Samurai cultures. As a side effect, their timely association advanced both the rise of Samurai hegemony and the spread of Zen philosophy in the national psyche. The abundant exchange between monk and warrior continued through the nineteenth century, at the close of Samurai rule. The Samurai government prevailed till 1867, when imperial authority was reestablished. By the mid-nineteenth century, Bushido standards had become the general ideal.

In 1871, the Samurai class was legally abolished, and the last four hundred thousand retainers were pensioned off and became *shizoku*, Japanese gentry. Most were absorbed into the civil service and business management. Five years later, it became illegal for anyone but the new national militia to wear a sword. After the emperor replaced feudal lords as the objects of military and public loyalty, Bushido became absorbed into the educational system of Japan. It was used to feed the rise of nationalism and strengthen civilian morale during World War II.

GLOSSARY

Bushi
Martial artist; warrior.

Bushido
Literally, "the way of the warrior"; the samurai code of chivalry. **Bukyou** is a term for "the teachings of Bushido."

Chanoyu
The tea ceremony.

Daimyo
A feudal samurai landowner and warlord.

Dojo
Literally, "a place to study the way"; a hall used for martial arts training.

Geta
Traditional wooden clogs. Geta are constructed of a single piece of wood, with vertical platforms carved into the sole to lift the wearer's feet above gravel, mud, ice, and snow.

Haiku
A seventeen-syllable poem, usually constructed in three lines of five, seven, and five syllables. Haiku

capture the mood of a fleeting moment, often through a reference to nature.

Koan

A Zen Buddhist question for deep introspection, designed to free the mind of its rigid adherence to conventional logic. Koan practice opens the practitioner to fresh dimensions of consciousness and experience. "What is the sound of one hand clapping?" is the most frequently quoted koan in the West.

Ronin

A lordless samurai.

Samurai (originally saburai)

Warrior; soldier.

Seiza

Literally, "correct sitting posture"; a kneeling position with the spine erect and hands folded over the thighs. While seiza is often used during public or religious events, and during tea ceremony (**chanoyu**), it is also a customary posture for some daily life activities in traditional Japanese households.

Sensei

Teacher. Great teachers are held in the highest regard for their capacity to transmit knowledge and catalyze tranformative growth in their students.

Seppuku

Ritual suicide by disembowelment. The term **hari-kiri** is better known in the West; however, in Japan, it is considered a more vulgar colloquialism for a very serious and deeply considered action.

Shogun

Military dictator of Japan; liege lord of the imperial court.

Shizoku

Professional gentry, such as civil servants and diplomatic attachés.

Tanka

A thirty-one-syllable poem, usually constructed in five lines of five, seven, five, seven, and seven syllables.

Tan T'ien

The center of balance in a human being, located about one and a half inches below the navel and an inch inside the lower abdomen. Through the use of breathing techniques such as Chi Kung and kundalini yoga, the Tan T'ien has potential to expand and deepen, and in doing so, help a person cultivate mental clarity, emotional depth, and spiritual awareness.

Tatami

Straw-wrapped padded floor covering. Tatami mats are

cool in summer, warm in winter, and provide comfortable support for sleeping, sitting, and the martial arts.

Zazen

Literally, "sitting Zen," zazen is the classic form of Zen meditation. Strict zazen is traditionally carried out in a cross-legged posture, seated on a floor cushion. However, some modern zendos (Zen schools) allow sitters to practice while seated on a stool or chair, or in the seiza posture.

For a comprehensive Japanese-English dictionary, visit the Japanese-English Dictionary Interface (JEDI) Web site: http://poets.notredame.ac.jp/cgi-bin/jedi-inon.